What's Going on Today?

Your Daily Planner and Journal

I0527658

Activinotes

Activinotes

DAILY JOURNALS, PLANNERS, NOTEBOOKS AND OTHER BLANK BOOKS

Daily Planner and Journal

notes

schedule

things to do

Daily Planner and Journal

notes

Daily Planner and Journal

notes

Daily Planner and Journal

notes

Daily Planner and Journal

notes

Daily Planner and Journal

notes

Daily Planner and Journal

schedule

things to do

notes

Daily Planner and Journal

notes

Daily Planner and Journal

notes

Daily Planner and Journal

notes

schedule

things to do

Daily Planner and Journal

notes

Daily Planner and Journal

notes

Daily Planner and Journal

notes

Daily Planner and Journal

notes

Daily Planner and Journal

notes

schedule

things to do

Daily Planner and Journal

notes

Daily Planner and Journal

notes

Daily Planner and Journal

notes

schedule

things to do

Daily Planner and Journal

notes

Daily Planner and Journal

notes

Daily Planner and Journal

notes

Daily Planner and Journal

notes

Daily Planner and Journal

notes

Daily Planner and Journal

notes

Daily Planner and Journal

notes

Daily Planner and Journal

notes

Daily Planner and Journal

notes

Daily Planner and Journal

notes

Daily Planner and Journal

notes

Daily Planner and Journal

notes

Daily Planner and Journal

schedule

things to do

notes

Daily Planner and Journal

notes

Daily Planner and Journal

notes

Daily Planner and Journal

notes

Daily Planner and Journal

notes

Daily Planner and Journal

schedule

things to do

notes

Daily Planner and Journal

notes

Daily Planner and Journal

notes

Daily Planner and Journal

notes

Daily Planner and Journal

notes

Daily Planner and Journal

notes

Daily Planner and Journal

notes

Daily Planner and Journal

notes

Daily Planner and Journal

notes

Daily Planner and Journal

notes

Daily Planner and Journal

notes

schedule

things to do

Daily Planner and Journal

notes

schedule

things to do

Daily Planner and Journal

notes

Daily Planner and Journal

notes

Daily Planner and Journal

schedule

things to do

notes

Daily Planner and Journal

notes

schedule

things to do

Daily Planner and Journal

notes

Daily Planner and Journal

notes

Daily Planner and Journal

notes

Daily Planner and Journal

Daily Planner and Journal

notes

Daily Planner and Journal

notes

Daily Planner and Journal

notes

Daily Planner and Journal

notes

Daily Planner and Journal

notes

Daily Planner and Journal

notes

Daily Planner and Journal

notes

Daily Planner and Journal

notes

schedule

things to do

Daily Planner and Journal

notes

Daily Planner and Journal

notes

Daily Planner and Journal

notes

Daily Planner and Journal

notes

Daily Planner and Journal

schedule

things to do

notes

Daily Planner and Journal

notes

Daily Planner and Journal

notes

Daily Planner and Journal

Daily Planner and Journal

notes

Daily Planner and Journal

notes

Daily Planner and Journal

schedule

things to do

notes

Daily Planner and Journal

notes

Daily Planner and Journal

notes

Daily Planner and Journal

notes

Daily Planner and Journal

notes

schedule

things to do

Daily Planner and Journal

notes

Daily Planner and Journal

notes

Daily Planner and Journal

notes

Daily Planner and Journal

notes

Daily Planner and Journal

notes

Daily Planner and Journal

notes

Daily Planner and Journal

notes

Daily Planner and Journal

notes

schedule

things to do

Daily Planner and Journal

notes

Daily Planner and Journal

notes

Daily Planner and Journal

schedule

things to do

notes

Daily Planner and Journal

notes

Daily Planner and Journal

notes

Daily Planner and Journal

schedule

things to do

notes

Daily Planner and Journal

notes

Daily Planner and Journal

notes

schedule

things to do

Daily Planner and Journal

notes

Daily Planner and Journal

notes

Daily Planner and Journal

notes

Daily Planner and Journal

notes

Daily Planner and Journal

schedule

things to do

notes

Daily Planner and Journal

notes

Daily Planner and Journal

notes

Daily Planner and Journal

schedule

things to do

notes

Daily Planner and Journal

notes

Daily Planner and Journal

notes

www.ingramcontent.com/pod-product-compliance
Lightning Source LLC
Chambersburg PA
CBHW080720290626
47170CB00017B/2867